Mel Bay Presents
Ancient & Modern Songs of Ireland for Piano

By Gail Smith

Cover Photo Credit: R. Kord/H. Armstrong Roberts

D1717254

A cassette tape of the music in this book is now available. The publisher strongly recommends the use of this cassette tape along with the text to insure accuracy of interpretation and ease in learning.

CONTENTS

Not included on recording.

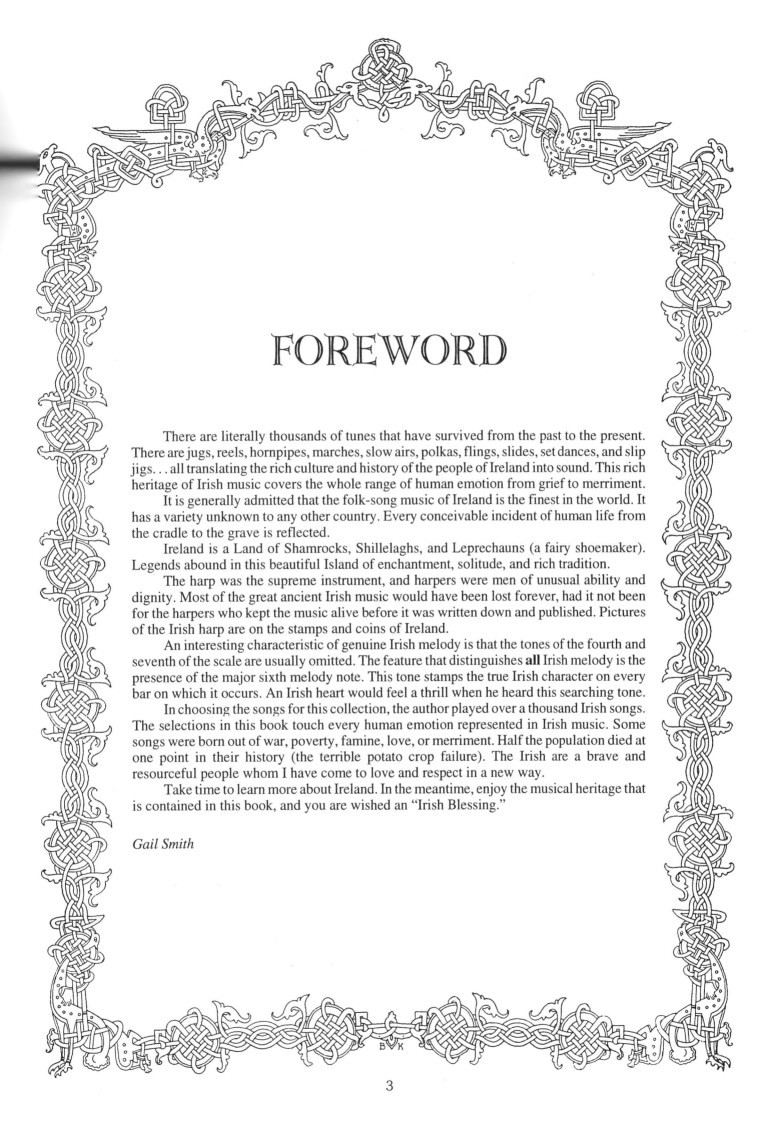

FOREWORD

There are literally thousands of tunes that have survived from the past to the present. There are jugs, reels, hornpipes, marches, slow airs, polkas, flings, slides, set dances, and slip jigs. . . all translating the rich culture and history of the people of Ireland into sound. This rich heritage of Irish music covers the whole range of human emotion from grief to merriment.

It is generally admitted that the folk-song music of Ireland is the finest in the world. It has a variety unknown to any other country. Every conceivable incident of human life from the cradle to the grave is reflected.

Ireland is a Land of Shamrocks, Shillelaghs, and Leprechauns (a fairy shoemaker). Legends abound in this beautiful Island of enchantment, solitude, and rich tradition.

The harp was the supreme instrument, and harpers were men of unusual ability and dignity. Most of the great ancient Irish music would have been lost forever, had it not been for the harpers who kept the music alive before it was written down and published. Pictures of the Irish harp are on the stamps and coins of Ireland.

An interesting characteristic of genuine Irish melody is that the tones of the fourth and seventh of the scale are usually omitted. The feature that distinguishes **all** Irish melody is the presence of the major sixth melody note. This tone stamps the true Irish character on every bar on which it occurs. An Irish heart would feel a thrill when he heard this searching tone.

In choosing the songs for this collection, the author played over a thousand Irish songs. The selections in this book touch every human emotion represented in Irish music. Some songs were born out of war, poverty, famine, love, or merriment. Half the population died at one point in their history (the terrible potato crop failure). The Irish are a brave and resourceful people whom I have come to love and respect in a new way.

Take time to learn more about Ireland. In the meantime, enjoy the musical heritage that is contained in this book, and you are wished an "Irish Blessing."

Gail Smith

THE RED-HAIRED GIRL

> This song is in honor of the famous early Queen of Ireland. Her name was Macha Mong Ruad (the red-haired). She reigned over the land about three hundred years before Christ. Her father, Aod Ruad, was one of the triumvirate. The others were Dithorba and Cimbaoth. They each took seven-year terms in reigning over Ireland. Aod Ruad drowned, so when his turn came around again, his daughter Macha claimed the crown.
>
> Macha had to fight her father's two partners. She had Dithorba killed, and she married Cimbaoth, making him King. The reign of Cimbaoth synchronizes with that of Alexander the Great. It marks the beginning of recorded Irish history.
>
> When Cimbaoth died, Macha took over the government, becoming the first Queen of Ireland.

F. O'Neil
Arr. by Gail Smith

THE HARP THAT ONCE THROUGH TARA'S HALLS

The great heart and center of the ancient Irish Kingdom was Tara. Five great roads radiated from Tara to the various parts of the country.

The greatest structure there was the Mi-Cuarta, the great banqueting hall. Hundreds of ancient poets sang of the greatness, glory, and luxury of Tara. In recent times, beautiful rare objects of gold have been dug up there as actual evidence of the past splendor.

Ollam Fodla first gave Tara historic fame by founding the Triennial Parliament there seven or eight centuries before Christ.

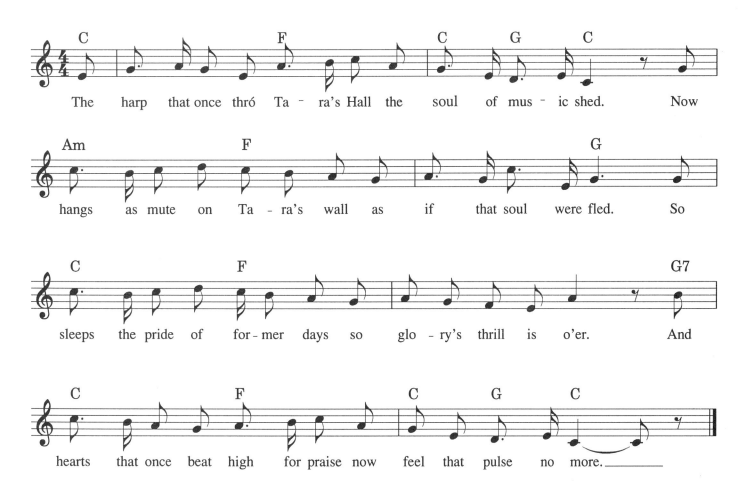

The harp that once thró Ta - ra's Hall the soul of mus - ic shed. Now

hangs as mute on Ta - ra's wall as if that soul were fled. So

sleeps the pride of for - mer days so glo - ry's thrill is o'er. And

hearts that once beat high for praise now feel that pulse no more._____

No more to chiefs and ladies bright, the harp of Tara swells
The chord alone, that breaks at night, it's tale of ruin tells
This freedom now so seldom wakes, the only throb she gives
Is when some heart indignant breaks, to show that still she lives.

THE HARP THAT ONCE THROUGH TARA'S HALLS

Thomas Moore
Arr. by Gail Smith

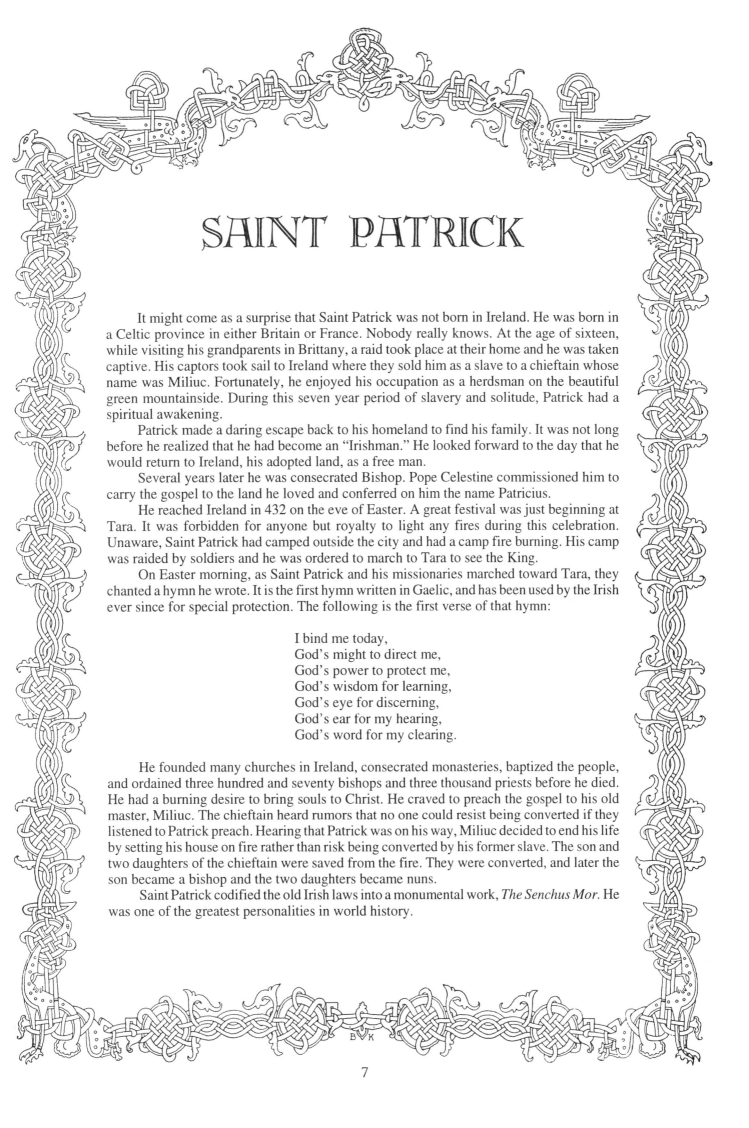

SAINT PATRICK

It might come as a surprise that Saint Patrick was not born in Ireland. He was born in a Celtic province in either Britain or France. Nobody really knows. At the age of sixteen, while visiting his grandparents in Brittany, a raid took place at their home and he was taken captive. His captors took sail to Ireland where they sold him as a slave to a chieftain whose name was Miliuc. Fortunately, he enjoyed his occupation as a herdsman on the beautiful green mountainside. During this seven year period of slavery and solitude, Patrick had a spiritual awakening.

Patrick made a daring escape back to his homeland to find his family. It was not long before he realized that he had become an "Irishman." He looked forward to the day that he would return to Ireland, his adopted land, as a free man.

Several years later he was consecrated Bishop. Pope Celestine commissioned him to carry the gospel to the land he loved and conferred on him the name Patricius.

He reached Ireland in 432 on the eve of Easter. A great festival was just beginning at Tara. It was forbidden for anyone but royalty to light any fires during this celebration. Unaware, Saint Patrick had camped outside the city and had a camp fire burning. His camp was raided by soldiers and he was ordered to march to Tara to see the King.

On Easter morning, as Saint Patrick and his missionaries marched toward Tara, they chanted a hymn he wrote. It is the first hymn written in Gaelic, and has been used by the Irish ever since for special protection. The following is the first verse of that hymn:

> I bind me today,
> God's might to direct me,
> God's power to protect me,
> God's wisdom for learning,
> God's eye for discerning,
> God's ear for my hearing,
> God's word for my clearing.

He founded many churches in Ireland, consecrated monasteries, baptized the people, and ordained three hundred and seventy bishops and three thousand priests before he died. He had a burning desire to bring souls to Christ. He craved to preach the gospel to his old master, Miliuc. The chieftain heard rumors that no one could resist being converted if they listened to Patrick preach. Hearing that Patrick was on his way, Miliuc decided to end his life by setting his house on fire rather than risk being converted by his former slave. The son and two daughters of the chieftain were saved from the fire. They were converted, and later the son became a bishop and the two daughters became nuns.

Saint Patrick codified the old Irish laws into a monumental work, *The Senchus Mor*. He was one of the greatest personalities in world history.

PATRICK'S DAY

A SONG WRITTEN IN HONOR OF ST. PATRICK'S DAY

Author and date unknown

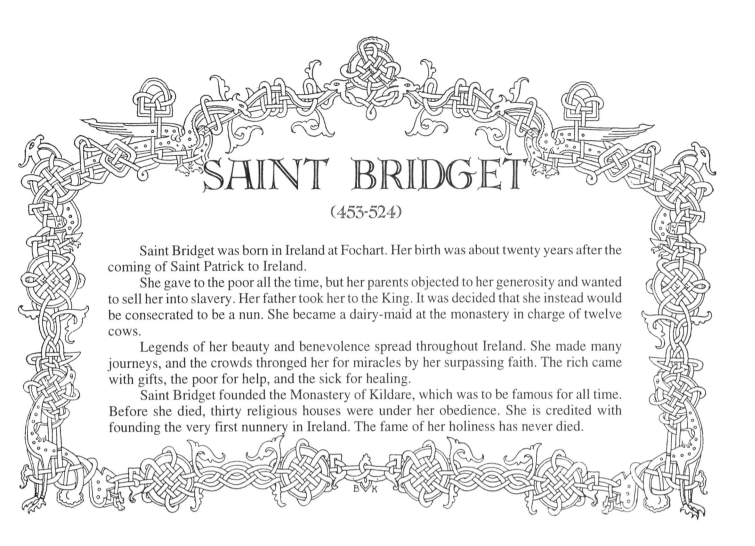

SAINT BRIDGET

(453-524)

Saint Bridget was born in Ireland at Fochart. Her birth was about twenty years after the coming of Saint Patrick to Ireland.

She gave to the poor all the time, but her parents objected to her generosity and wanted to sell her into slavery. Her father took her to the King. It was decided that she instead would be consecrated to be a nun. She became a dairy-maid at the monastery in charge of twelve cows.

Legends of her beauty and benevolence spread throughout Ireland. She made many journeys, and the crowds thronged her for miracles by her surpassing faith. The rich came with gifts, the poor for help, and the sick for healing.

Saint Bridget founded the Monastery of Kildare, which was to be famous for all time. Before she died, thirty religious houses were under her obedience. She is credited with founding the very first nunnery in Ireland. The fame of her holiness has never died.

YOUNG BRIDGET

F. O'Neil

YOUNG BRIDGET

Very Ancient, Author and date unknown

THERE WAS A YOUNG LADY

Very Ancient, Author and date unknown

In moderate time

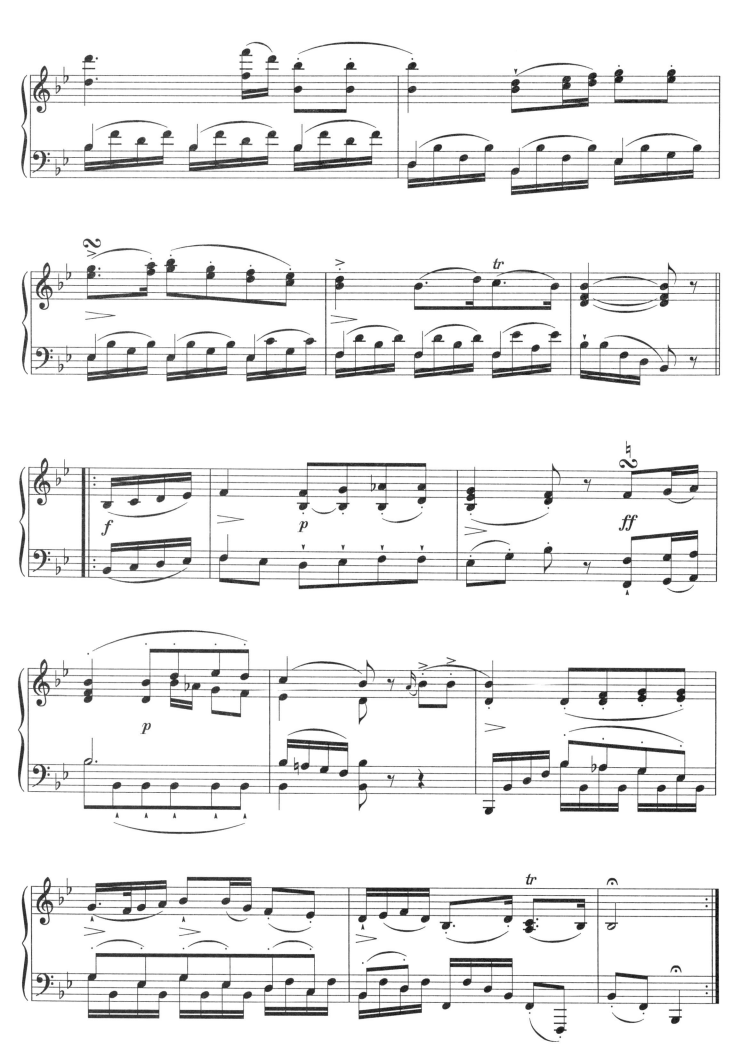

A CHIEFTAIN

Arranged by
Gail Smith

EDWARD BUNTING

(1773-1843)

Edward Bunting was a preserver of the music of Ireland. He organized the Harp Festival of 1792 held in Belfast. The object was to bring together the old harpers, and have them all play the ancient tunes and airs as they remembered them. An attempt was made to hear the traditional tunes played by ten of the most qualified harpers. The tunes were collected and taken down by Edward Bunting as the harpers played and played and played on their harps.

After the festival was over, Edward Bunting studied the tunes and then compiled, edited, and published two volumes of the ancient airs and traditional tunes of the day, for posterity.

At the famous meeting, certain tunes had to be played according to regulation: "Coolin," "The Dawning of the Day," and "Ellen a Roon."

The following selections include some of the songs that you would have heard if you had attended that festival two hundred years ago.

FEAGHAN GELEASH

(OR TRY IF IT IS IN TUNE)

This is an extremely ancient and curious Irish prelude. It was taken down by Edward Bunting in 1792, as the harpist, Hempson, played it at the Belfast Festival. It was with great reluctance that the old harper was prevailed on to play this fragment preserved here. Hempson said that to play this air awakened recollections of the days of his youth, and of friends he had outlived.

It was the custom for one harper to play the ancient lamentation and then another harper to answer by playing the other half. When Edward Bunting pressed Hempson to play it he answered, "What's the use of doing so? No one can understand it now, not even any of the harpers now living."

This is but one half of the prelude. Hempson said he forgot the other half. We will never know. This is definitely one of the oldest Irish tunes, if not **the oldest**.

An Ancient Prelude for the Harp

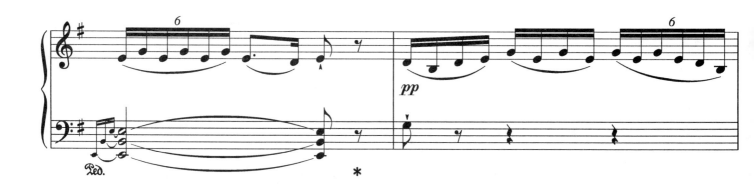

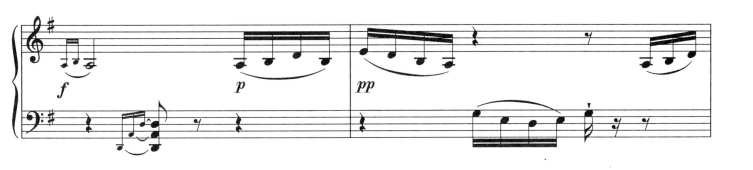

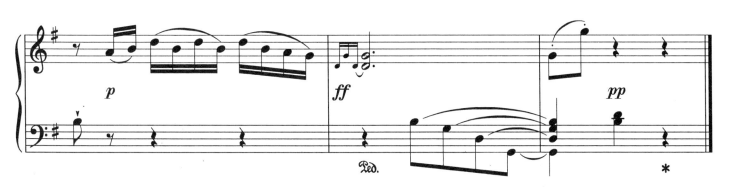

SCOTT'S LAMENTATION

AS ORIGINALLY PERFORMED BY HEMPSON ON THE IRISH HARP

Leading sinews
or preparatory notes

Composed in 1599

THE RIDDLE SONG

(GO NO MORE A RUSHING)

> This is a riddle-song, one of the most ancient types of folk-song. It is a dialogue-type song which can be traced back to the 15th century.
>
> The traditional plot is that a maiden is accosted by the devil, disguised as an earthling. To escape his power she must solve the seemingly impossible riddle.

The Riddle Song

How can there be a cherry without a stone?
How can there be a chicken without a bone?
How can there be a ring that has no rim at all?
How can there be a bird that hasn't got a gall?
When the cherry's in the flower it has no stone,
When the chicken's in the egg it has no bone.
When the ring is in the making it has no rim at all,
And the dove is a bird with out a gall.

Arr. by Gail Smith

21

ELLEN A ROONE

Very Ancient, Author and date unknown
Varied by LYONS in 1702

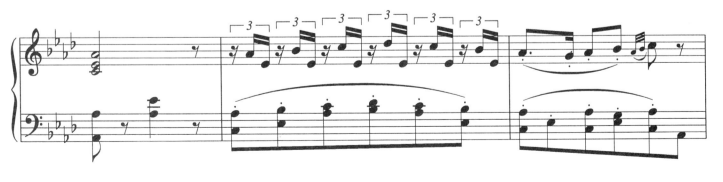

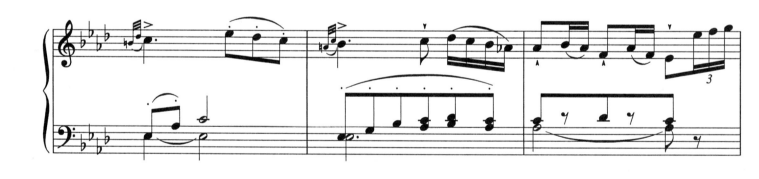

COOEE EN DEVENISH

(OR THE LAMENTATION OF YOUTHS)

Composed by HARRY SCOTT in 1603,
for HUSSEY, Baron of Galtrim

**Rather Quick
and distinctly**

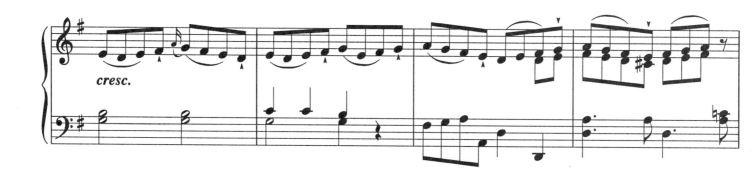

JACKSON'S MORNING BRUSH

Composed by JACKSON about 1776

Lively and Animated

28

COOLIN

(OR LADY OF THE DESERT)

Very Ancient, Author and date unknown
With Variations by LYONS in the year 1702

VAR: 2nd
Slow and
Plaintive

Very soft

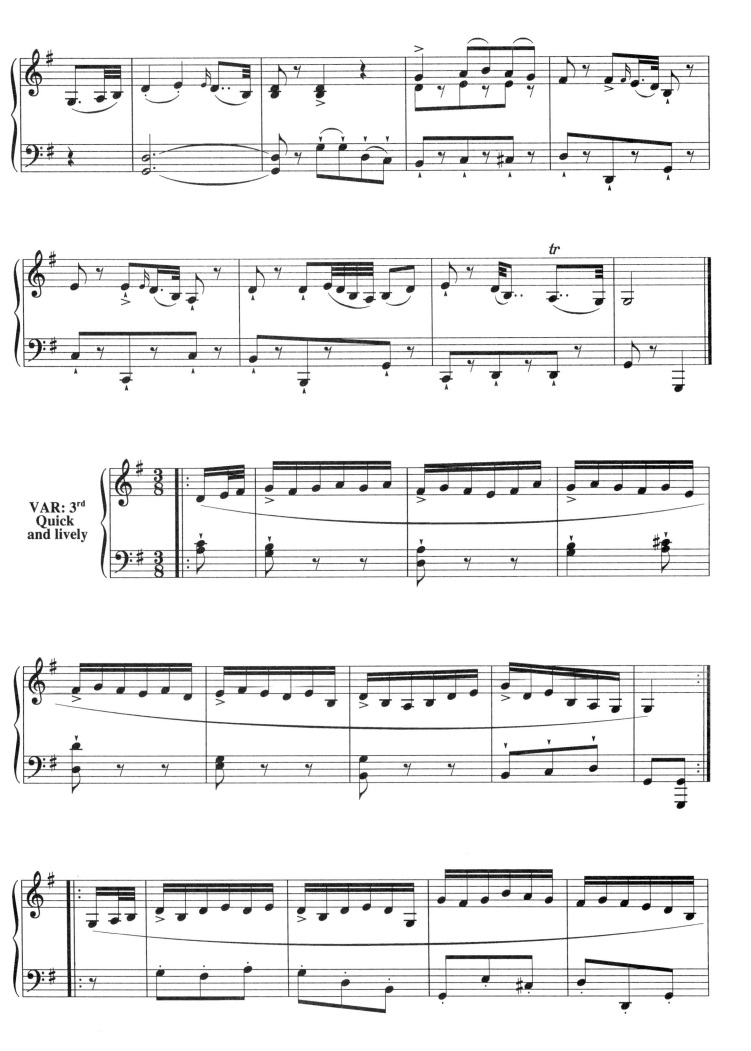

VAR: 3rd
Quick
and lively

33

VAR: 4th Slower.

Very soft

ten.

tr

ten.

tr

tr

34

THE GENTLE MAIDEN

Very Ancient, Author and date unknown

Very Slow and with great Expression

BLACK ROSE BUD

Very Ancient, Author and date unknown

A little slow

The Arpeggios as originally played by the Harpers.

SECOND SET OF
BLACK ROSE BUD

Very Ancient, Author & date unknown

Rather slow

YOURSELF ALONG WITH ME

Very Ancient, Author and date unknown

THE HARE IN THE CORN

This piece was an ancient tune for the pipes, in which there is an imitation of a hunt, including the sound of the horn of the huntsmen, the crying of the dogs, and finally the death of the hare. This performance can only be properly given on the pipes. The principal tube, when pressed with its lower end against the leather guard on the performer's knee, can be made to yield a smothered, sobbing tone, very much like the sound of a cry of the hare. This would be most difficult to describe in musical notation.

Author and date unknown

With spirit

HEALTH FROM THE CUP

Very Ancient, Author and date unknown

PADDY O RAFFERTY

Author and date unknown

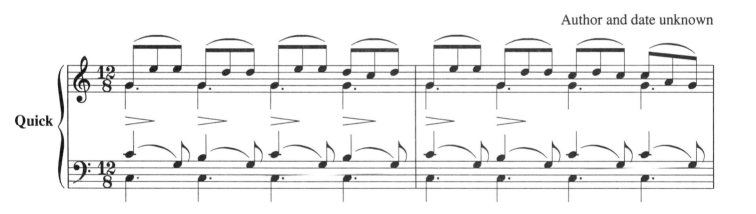

43

THE BONNY CUCKOO

Very Ancient, Author and date unknown

Cheerful and tenderly

My Bonny Cuc koo I tell thee true That through the groves I'll rove with you I'll rove with you un - till the next spring And then my Cuc-koo shall sweet - ly sing Cuc - koo - Cuc - koo - un - till the next spring And then my Cuc-koo shall sweet - ly sing.

The Ash and the Hazel shall mourning say,
My bonny Cuckoo don't go away,
Don't go away but tarry here,
And make the season last all the year.

SWEET PORTAFERRY

Very Ancient, Author and date unknown

THE YELLOW BLANKET

Very Ancient,
Author and date unknown

THE ROBBER

(OR CHARLEY REILLY)

Very Ancient,
Author and date unknown

Moderately Quick

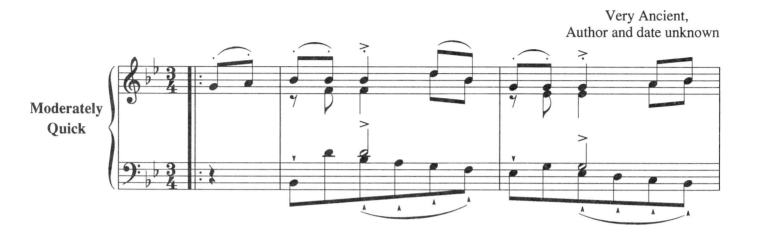

SIT DOWN UNDER MY PROTECTION

Very Ancient,
Author and date unknown

Moderately Quick

THE JOLLY PLOUGHMAN

Very Ancient,
Author and date unknown

JACK he sung his song so sweet he made the val - lies

Chorus:

ring. With his Too - ran - nan nan - ty na sing.

Too - ran - nan nan - ty na sing Too - ran - nan Too - ran - nan

Too - ran - nan Too - ran - nan Too - ran - nan nan - ty na.

THE HURLER'S MARCH

(KING'S COUNTY)

Very Ancient,
Author and date unknown

**With Life
and Spirit**

THE BROWN AND WHITE GARLAND

Very Ancient,
Author and date unknown

**Rather Slow
and
Gracefully**

SOFT MILD MORNING

Very Ancient,
Author and date unknown

IF I HAD A COURT AND CASTLE

Author and date unknown

**Moderately
Quick and
Cheerful**

BONNY PORTMORE

Very Ancient, Author and date unknown

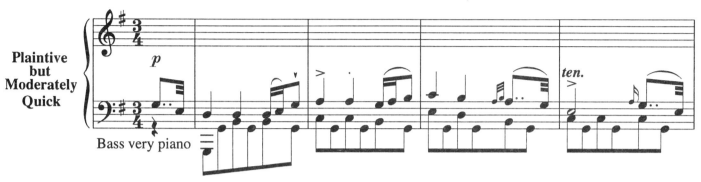

Plaintive but Moderately Quick

Bass very piano

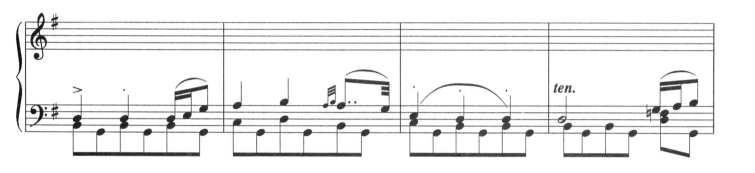

Bass well marked

THE WHITE CALF

Very Ancient, Author and date unknown

THE REJECTED LOVER

Author and date unknown

Moderately Lively

PREPARING TO SAIL AWAY

Very Ancient,
Author and date unknown

**Distinctly
and
Moderately**

THE BLACK HAIRED GIRL

Very Ancient,
Author and date unknown

**Lively
and
Animated**

'TIS A PITY I DON'T
SEE MY LOVE

Very Ancient, Author and date unknown

THE KILKENNY TUNE

Author and date unknown

In
marching time

IS IT THE PRIEST YOU WANT?

Very Ancient, Author and date unknown

I'LL FOLLOW YOU OVER THE MOUNTAIN

Allegretto

A DEATH SONG

THE BUTTERFLY

Andante

THE WREN

Andante Grazioso

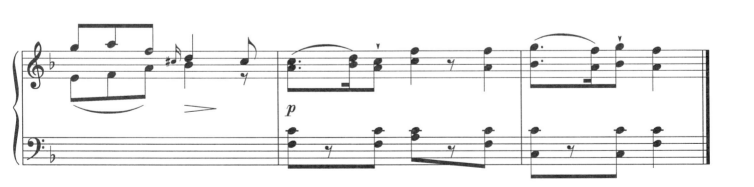

THE BLACKBIRD

Very Ancient, Author and date unknown

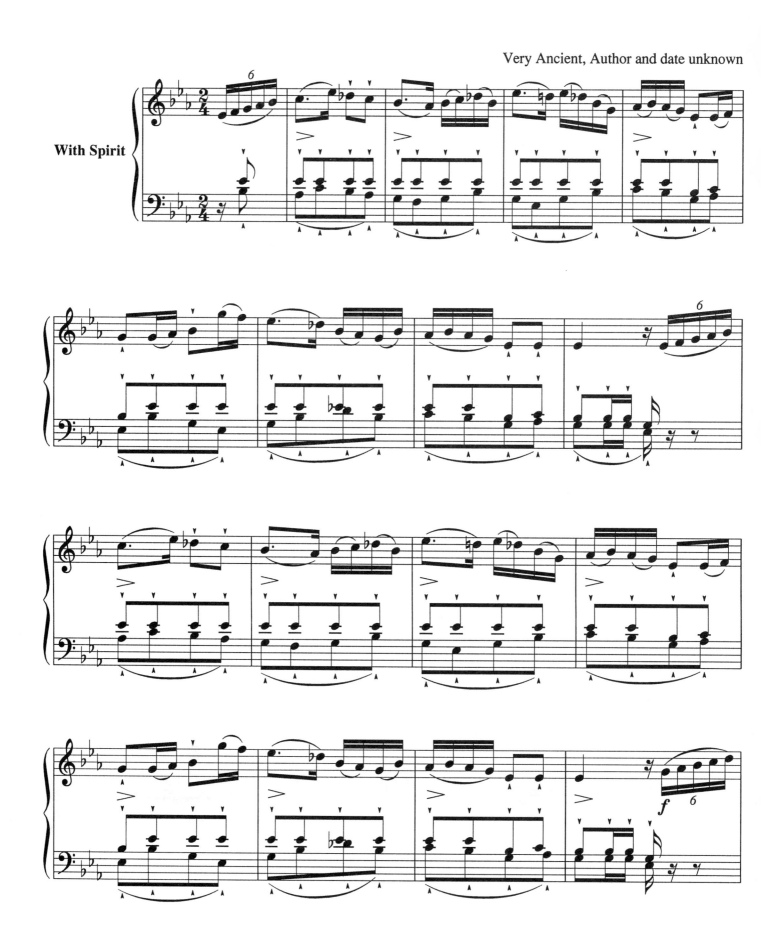

With Spirit

THE LITTLE SWALLOW

Very Ancient, Author and date unknown

Tenderly and in a singing style

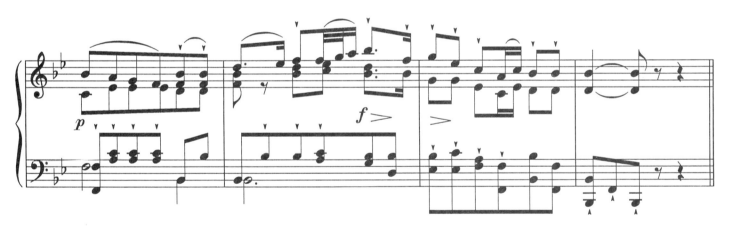

TIE THE RIBBONS

(REEL)

Mrs. Cantwell
Arranged by Gail Smith

SPINNING WHEEL SONG

What's the noise that I hear at the window I wonder,
'Tis the little birds chirping the holly - bush under'
'What makes you be shoving and moving your stool on,
An' singing, all wrong, that old song of "The Coolun"?

There's a form at the casement, - the form of her true - love,
And he whispers, with face bent: 'I'm waiting for you love.
Get up from the stool, through the lattice step lightly,
We'll rove in the grove while the moon's shining brightly'.

Merrily, cheerily, noiselessly whirring,
Spins the wheel, rings the wheel, while the foot's stirring,
Sprightly and lightly and airily ringing,
Trills the sweet voice of the young maiden singing.

SPINNING WHEEL SONG

Allegro

Arr. by Gail Smith

bring out melody

CHORUS JIG

The "Chorus Jig" is an Irish melody whose date and authorship are unknown. This melody has always been a favorite with pipers. Jigs were originally tunes sung by clowns after the play. In the 17th century everyone sang them, and the dances were known as Irish jigs.

Arranged by Gail Smith

THRESHING THE BARLEY

In Ireland, as in all parts of the world, the value of music as an aid and stimulus to work is attested to overwhelmingly.

There is a great variety of occupational tunes, such as for milking, spinning, and plowing. The next two songs are such examples.

THRESHING THE BARLEY

Arr. by Gail Smith

83

THE SPINNER'S DELIGHT

J. O'Neil
Arr. by Gail Smith

THREE LOOBEENS

The loobeen is a peculiar species of chaunt, having a well marked time, and a frequently recurring chorus or catch-word. It is accompanied by extemporaneous verses, of which each singer successively furnishes a line. The Loobeen goes round until the chain of song is completed.

These songs were sung at "quilting" parties. It is interesting to note that the Double Irish Chain is a universally know quilt pattern. Within the open spaces formed by the chain, the quilters often appliqued or embroidered a design. They were very popular in the late 1800s and early 1900s.

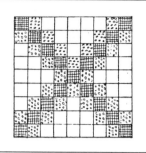

Very Ancient,
Author and date unknown

HAMPSON HEMPSON
He lived to the astounding age of 112, playing his harp up to the day before his death.

THE IRISH WASHERWOMAN

This is an old Irish reel that was published in 1688, known as "The Country Courtship." The Virginia Reel is a survival of a dance of the crafts. It is an imitation of weaving—one figure representing the shuttle that moves through the warp and woof of thread.

Arr. by Gail Smith

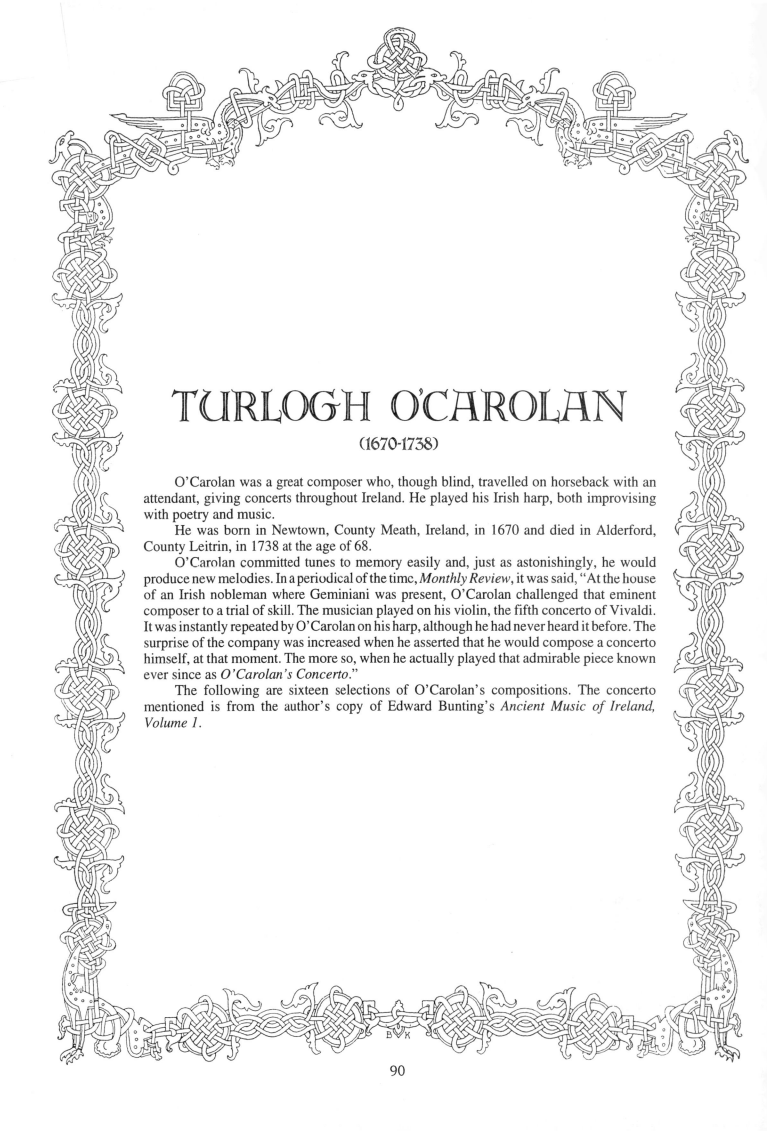

TURLOGH O'CAROLAN

(1670-1738)

O'Carolan was a great composer who, though blind, travelled on horseback with an attendant, giving concerts throughout Ireland. He played his Irish harp, both improvising with poetry and music.

He was born in Newtown, County Meath, Ireland, in 1670 and died in Alderford, County Leitrin, in 1738 at the age of 68.

O'Carolan committed tunes to memory easily and, just as astonishingly, he would produce new melodies. In a periodical of the time, *Monthly Review*, it was said, "At the house of an Irish nobleman where Geminiani was present, O'Carolan challenged that eminent composer to a trial of skill. The musician played on his violin, the fifth concerto of Vivaldi. It was instantly repeated by O'Carolan on his harp, although he had never heard it before. The surprise of the company was increased when he asserted that he would compose a concerto himself, at that moment. The more so, when he actually played that admirable piece known ever since as *O'Carolan's Concerto*."

The following are sixteen selections of O'Carolan's compositions. The concerto mentioned is from the author's copy of Edward Bunting's *Ancient Music of Ireland, Volume 1*.

THE PRINCESS ROYAL

By O'Carolan

Rather Slow and Moderately

O'CAROLAN'S CONCERTO

By O'Carolan

MRS. CROFTON

By O'Carolan

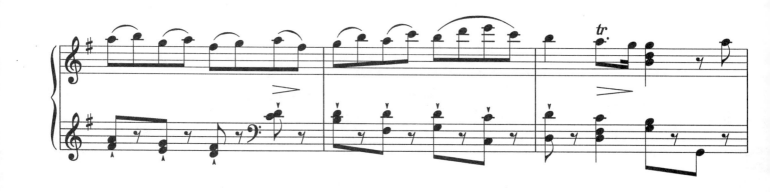

SIR FESTUS BURKE

By O'Carolan

LADY BLANEY

By O'Carolan

Moderately
Quick and
Lively

Original Harp Bass

O'CAROLAN'S DEVOTION

Comp. about 1700

In an animated style

O'CAROLAN'S RECEIPT

(OR STAFFORD'S RECEIPT OF WHISKEY)

Comp. about 1725

103

DOCTOR JOHN HART

By O'Carolan

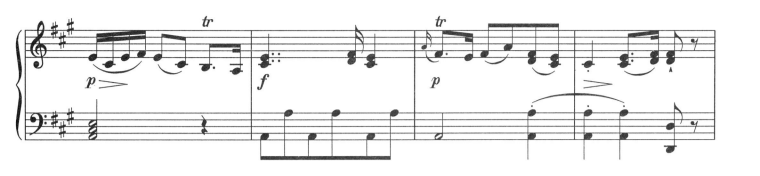

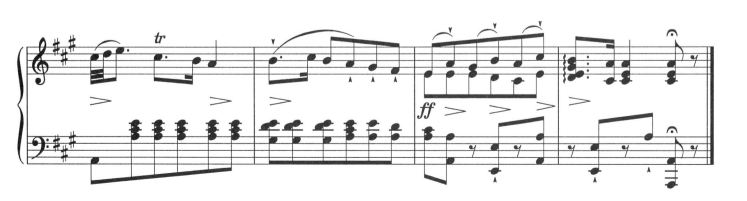

PLANGSTY CHARLES COOTE

By O'Carolan

TOBY PEYTON'S PLANGSTY

By O'Carolan

Brisk and Lively

FANNY POWER

By O'Carolan

**Distinctly
and
gracefully**

108

MADAM MAXWELL

By O'Carolan

A LESSON FOR THE HARP

By O'Carolan

Allegro

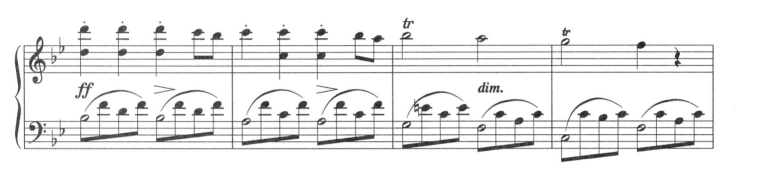

PLANGSTY HUGH O'DONNELL

By O'Carolan

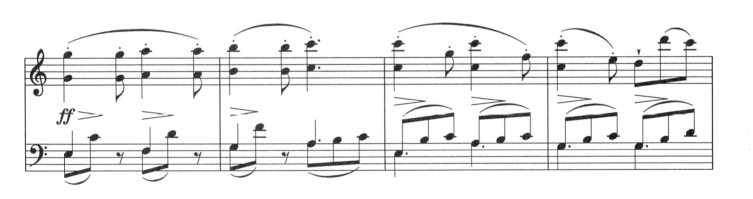

O'CAROLAN'S LAMENT

Arranged by Gail Smith

114

PLANGSTY BURKE

By O'Carolan

Very Quick

IRISH GIRL

The words to this song are:
"You are the fairest of Irish maidens,
And you are fit, love, to be a queen.
I wish I was in some battle wounded
Before your sweet pretty face I'd seen."

Arranged by Gail Smith

THE LAST ROSE OF SUMMER

This lovely song is dedicated to the rose, considered to be the most beautiful flower in the world. The poem was written by Thomas Moore (1779-1852). The tune is the familiar "Grooves of Blarney."

Tis the last rose of Sum - mer_____ left - blo - om - ing all a - lone._____ All her love - ly com - pan - ions_____ are - fa - - ded and gone._____ No_ flow - er of her kin - dred,_____ no - rose bud_____ is neigh, to re - flect back her_ blush - es_____ and _ gi - ve sigh for sigh._____

'Tis the last rose of summer, left blooming alone.
All her lovely companions are faded and gone.
No Flower of her kindred, no rose bud is nigh.
To reflect back her blushes or give sigh for sigh.

I'll not leave thee, thou lone one! to pine on the stem.
Since the lovely are sleeping, go, sleep thou with them.
Thus kindly I scatter thy leaves o'er the bed
Where thy mates of the garden lie scentless and dead.

So soon may I follow, when friendships decay.
And from love's shining circle the gems drop away.
When true hearts lie wither'd and fond ones are flown,
Oh! who would inhabit this bleak world alone!

THE LAST ROSE OF SUMMER

Air: The Groves of Blarney
Arranged by Gail Smith

Andante expressivo

119

OFT, IN THE STILLY NIGHT

Oft in the stil - ly night ere slum - bers chain has bound ___ me.

Fond mem - ory brings the light of ___ ot - her days a - round me. The

smiles, the tears of boy - hood years the words of love then spok - en ___ The

eyes that shone now dimmed and gone the cheer - ful hearts now broken ___

Thus in the stil - ly night ere slum - bers chain has bound ___ me.

Sad mem - ory brings the light of - ot - her days a - round me.

Oft, in the stilly night,
  Ere Slumber's chain has bound me,
Fond memory brings the light
  Of other days around me.
The smiles, the tears, of boyhood's years,
The words of love then spoken;
The eyes that shone,
  Now dimmed and gone,
The cheerful hearts now broken!
Thus, in the stilly night,
Ere Slumber's chain hath bound me,
  Of other days around me.

When I remember all
  The friends, so linked together,
I've seen around me fall,
  Like leaves in wintry weather.
I feel like one, who treads alone,
Some banquet-hall deserted,
Whose lights are fled,
  Whose garlands dead,
And all but he departed!
Thus, in the stilly night,
  Ere Slumber's chain has bound me,
Sad memory brings the light
  Of other days around me.

OFT, IN THE STILLY NIGHT

Thomas Moore
Arranged by Gail Smith

THE PRETTY GIRL MILKING HER COW

Air: Cailin Deas
Arranged by Gail Smith

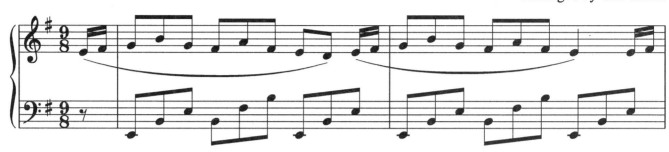

BELIEVE ME, IF ALL THOSE ENDEARING YOUNG CHARMS

This lovely song was written by the famous poet Thomas Moore at a time when his wife was suffering from a skin disease. She feared he would no longer love her. He wrote this tender song and dedicated it to her.

It is not while beauty and youth are thine own
And thy cheeks unprofaned by a tear
That the fervour and faith of a soul can be known
To which time will but make thee more dear.
No, the heart that has truly loved never forgets
But as truly loves on to the close
As the sun-flower turns on her God when he sets
The same look which she turned when he rose.

BELIEVE ME, IF ALL THOSE
ENDEARING YOUNG CHARMS

Thomas Moore
Arranged by Gail Smith

124

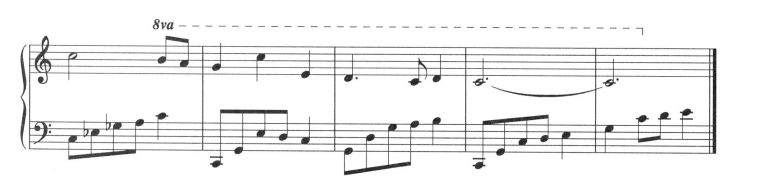

THE WILD GEESE

The "Wild Geese" refers to the Irish Brigade (1691-1740) who served with the French, hoping to drive the English out of Ireland.

Very Ancient, Auther and date unknown

CHORUS

GREEN SLEEVES

(DOUBLE JIG)

The earliest reference written to validate "Green Sleeves" was in 1580. There are many versions of the lyrics; however, the best known is probably the Christmas carol, "What Child is This?"

Arranged by Gail Smith

Moderato

130

SALLY GARDENS

A *sally* is a willow tree. This poem was written by William Butler Yeats, and first published in the volume *Crossways* in 1889. Herbert Hughes, the famous folk-song singer/scholar, set it to this old Irish air.

Down by the ___ Sal - ly ___ gar - dens, my ___ love and ___ I did meet, She ___

passed the ___ Sal - ly ___ gar - dens, with ___ lit - tle ___ snow - white feet, She

bid me: ___ 'Take love ea - sy, as the leaves grow ___ on ___ the ___ tree.' But ___

I, be - ing young and ___ fool - ish, with ___ her did ___ not a - gree.

In a field down by the river my love and I did stand
And on my leaning shoulder, she laid her snow-white hand
She bid me take life easy, as the grass grows on the weirs;
But I was young and foolish and now am full of tears.

Down by the sally gardens, my love and I did meet;
She passed the sally gardens, with little snow-white feet.
She bid me take love easy, as the leaves grow on the tree;
But I being young and foolish, with her did not agree.

SALLY GARDENS

Arranged by Gail Smith

COCKLES AND MUSSELS

The rivers Shannon, Lee, and Boyne, which flow through Ireland, are full of salmon, and the lakes and streams are full of trout. The fresh fish, cockles, and mussels were sold from wicker three-wheeled carts in the cities. Of course, all true Irishmen had fish on Fridays.

She was a fishmonger
But sure 'twas no wonder
For so were her father and mother before,
And they both wheeled their barrow
Through streets broad and narrow.
Crying cockles and mussels,
    alive, alive, oh!

Repeat Chorus

She died of a fever
And no one could save her
And that was the end of sweet Molly Malone.
But her ghost wheels her barrow
Through streets broad and narrow.
Crying cockles and mussels
    alive, alive, oh!

Repeat Chorus

COCKLES AND MUSSELS

Arranged by Gail Smith

THE WEARING OF THE GREEN

Some have said that this is the real "national anthem of Ireland." Napper Tandy was an Irish patriot who was forced to flee the country in 1793 in order to save his life.

Here are the words to the anonymous street version of the song, dating back to 1798.

Dion Boucicault

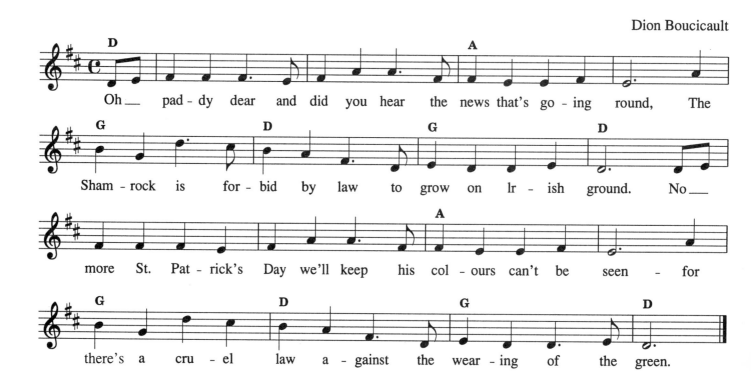

Oh — pad-dy dear and did you hear the news that's go-ing round, The Sham-rock is for-bid by law to grow on Ir-ish ground. No — more St. Pat-rick's Day we'll keep his col-ours can't be seen - for there's a cru-el law a-gainst the wear-ing of the green.

Oh! Paddy dear and did you hear the
   news that's going round,
The Shamrock is forbid by law to grow
   on Irish ground.
No more St. Patrick's Day we'll keep, his
   colours can't be seen,
For there's a cruel law against the
   wearing of the Green.
I met with Napper Tandy, and he took
   me by the hand,
And he said, "How's poor old Ireland
   and how does she stand?"
She's the most distressful country that
   ever yet was seen,
For they're hangin' men an' women for
   the wearing of the Green.

And if the colour we must wear is
   England's cruel Red,
Let it remind us of the blood that
   Ireland has shed.
Then pull the shamrock from your hat,
   and throw it on the sod,
And never fear, 'twill take root there,
   tho' under foot 'tis trod.
When the law can stop the blades of grass,
   from growing as they grow,
And when the leaves in summer-time
   their colour dare not show.
Then I will change the colour, too, I
   wear in my caubeen,
But 'till that day, please God, I'll stick
   to wearing of the Green.

THE WEARING OF THE GREEN

Arranged by Gail Smith

THE MINSTREL BOY

This battle song was written by Thomas Moore. It is sung to the air of "The Moreen."

The Min - strel boy___ to the war has gone in the ranks of death___ you will

find him. His fa - ther's sword he has gir - ded on and his wild harp slung___ be _

hind him. Land of song said the warr - ior bard though

all the world be - tray___ thee. One sword at least___ thy___

rights shall guard one___ faith - ful harp___ shall___ praise thee.

The Minstrel fell! - But the foeman's chain
Could not bring his proud soul under.
The harp he lov'd Ne'er spoke again
For he tore its chords asunder.
And said, "No chains shall sully thee
Thou soul of love and bravery!
Thy songs were made for the pure and free
They shall never sound in slavery".

THE MINSTREL BOY

Air: The Moreen
Arranged by Gail Smith

COLONEL O HARA

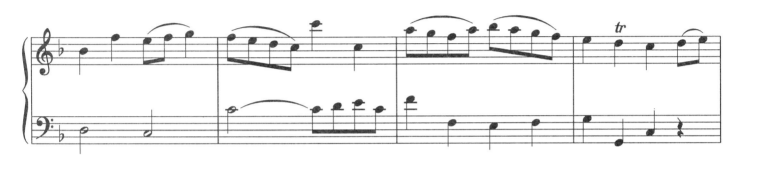

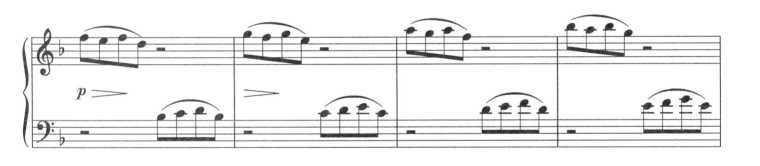

COLONEL IRWIN

DANNY BOY

And when ye come and all the flowers are dying,
If I am dead, as dead I well may be.
You'll come and find the place where I am lying,
And kneel and say an Ave there for me.

And I shall hear tho' soft you tread above me,
And all my grave will warmer, sweeter be
If you will bend and tell me that you love me,
Then I shall sleep in peace until you come to me.

LONDONDERRY AIR

(ALSO KNOWN AS DANNY BOY)

Irish music was absorbed into the American mainstream in the mid-nineteenth century, when over thirteen million immigrants arrived from Ireland.

Percy Grainger arranged and popularized this Irish tune.

Slowly, with feeling

Arranged by Gail Smith

IRISH LULLABY

Andante expressivo

Arranged by Gail Smith

146

THE GREY OLD STONE

This song refers to the blarney stone which is a non-descript block of limestone about four feet long, one foot wide, and nine inches high. The stone is said to be worth millions of dollars. Each year thousands of blarney believers climb 120 feet in search of "blarney" and hang upside down to kiss the stone.

Arr. by Gail Smith

Andante espressivo

WHEN IRISH EYES ARE SMILING

Words by CHAUNCEY OLCOTT and GEO GRAFF JNR
Music by ERNEST BALL

For your smile is a part, of the love in your heart,
And it makes even sunshine more bright
Like the linnet's sweet song, crooning all the day long,
Comes your laughter so tender and light.

For the spring - time of life is the sweetest of all,
There is ne'er a real care or regret;
And while spring-time is ours, throughout all of youth's hours,
Let us smile each chance we get.

WHEN IRISH EYES ARE SMILING

Arranged by Gail Smith

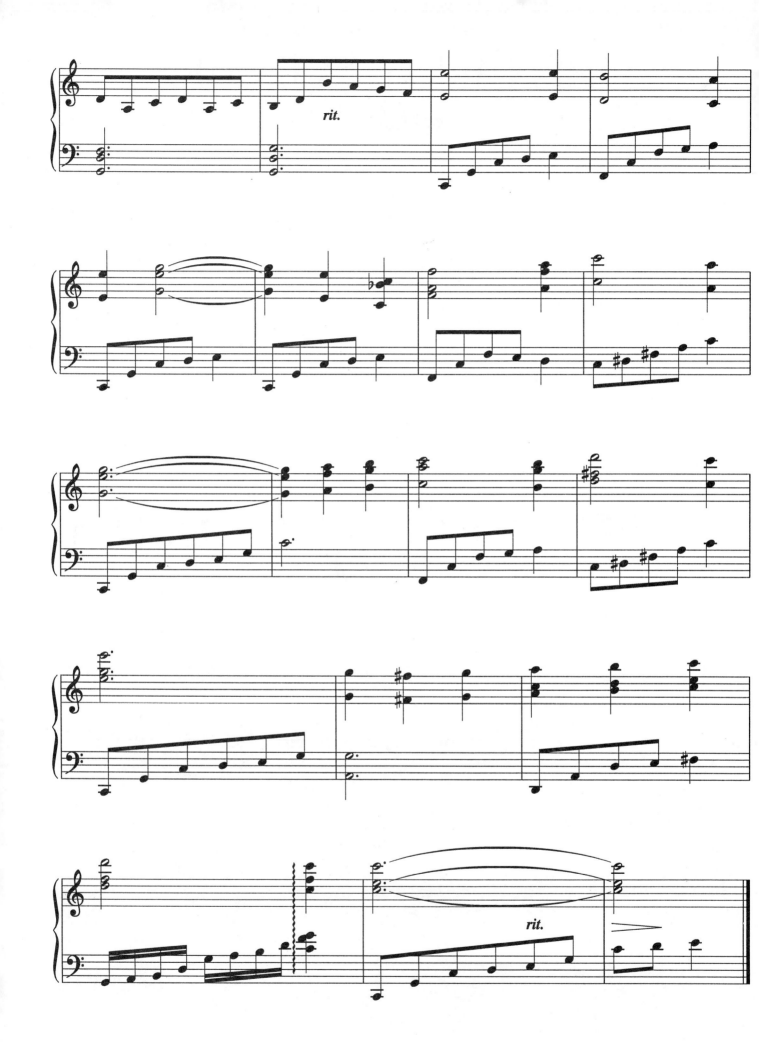